Introduction

A dictionary definition of a GRID is a network of evenly spaced horizontal and vertical lines, a set of crisscrossing bars. or a placement of squares formed within horizontal and vertical lines. However, in this book the term grid will be broadened to include asymmetrical arrangements of crossing lines and organic structures usually accepted within design terminology.

Consider the many elements that surround you in everyday life. Grids feature everywhere! For example, the street plans of many towns and cities are built in grid formations. Some grid patterns are more obvious such as those found on walls, fences, railings and the dozens to be featured on buildings. Focused looking will reveal many more.

Supermarkets stack their products on shelves displaying an array of multi coloured packets, tins and bottles. The fruit and vegetable sections are particularly colourful. The resulting patterns, textures and colours are shown in such a way to present the products and tempt the buyer to purchase. These displays could easily inspire new colour schemes and simplified or stylised patterns. Focus in on a pineapple or a husked sweet corn and marvel at their intricate structures. Some fruit and vegetables are also packed in plastic or foam containers to show the product as its supposed best. These preformed trays can be intriguing in their own right.

The same elements with infinite variations can be found in garden centres. Rows of hanging baskets, trays of small alpines, herbs or patio plants, many of which are grown in a vast array of varying coloured preformed plastic containers could all start an inspiring train of design thoughts. Look closely at cacti as many have regular, indented or dimensional grid patterning with impressive spikes.

Museums contain a wealth of inspiring grids within the artefacts on display.
Enjoy the multi coloured decorations painted on coffins of Egyptian mummies or Maori cloaks elaborately interwoven with pigeon and parrot feathers creating lines of triangular patterns. Tapa or bark cloths from Samoa or mud cloths from Africa are painted and decorated with exciting motifs, simple but most effective.
American Indian baskets are a joy to see, exhibiting wonderful designs in rich, subtle colours. In contrast, imposing Assyrian stone sculptures include stylised decorative bands within their headdresses, hair, beards and the borders on their robes.

Focusing on nature will also reveal stimulating features. Look carefully at the colours and patterns to be seen within butterfly wings, fish scales, seashells, and rock strata to mention just a few. Observing landscape from the air is totally absorbing too. Fields of crops, olive groves, vineyards and irrigation channels may suggest alternative designs ideas.

Spend some time looking at old photographs or sketchbooks for grid arrangements. Not only will this stimulate many memories of places visited but may well reveal fresh responses and details of places long forgotten. Allow time for reflection and jot down any additional information remembered.

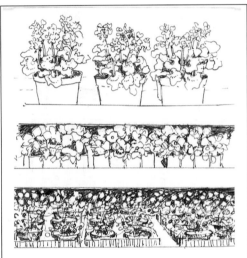

Although controversial, the elegant metal cages enclosing tiny birds in a market, boxes of appetising Turkish delight, rows of mouth watering patisseries and displays of iridescent shells seen in Paris set off a number of thoughts. Alternatively, the grid arrangement of oyster beds in Cancale in France, the spectacular mosaics in the Allambra Palace in Spain and a fabulous array of colourful chillies and pumpkins seen in Australia continue to inspire.

Many memories can be unearthed to relish and enjoy by going back a number of years and applying a singular focus. They could inspire renewed research leading to a reinvigorated approach to the work process.

Grids and Soluble Fabric

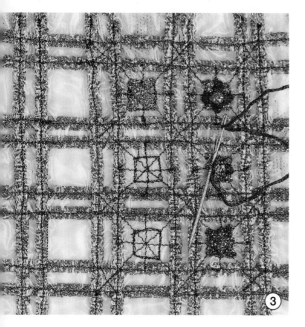

③

'Aquabond' ('Avalon Fix') is a comparatively new soluble fabric with a sticky surface. It has been successfully used in all the samples illustrated where a new cloth has been created using the dissolvable technique. Similar fabrics are available around the world but sold under other brand names. Trials with these would need to be completed before embarking on any major project.

The sticky side of the 'Aquabond' or 'Avalon fix' fabric is covered with a silicone coated paper to protect the adhesive surface. The actual material behaves in a similar way to 'Solusheet' but with the addition of the sticky surface. Handled with care, this product offers new opportunities and the overall structure of a picture or pattern can be easily built up at one time. The possibilities are truly exciting.

Initially the paper covering is peeled off to reveal the sticky surface. Great care needs to be taken at this stage. It is helpful to remember to carry out this action slowly. Gently peel back the paper little by little, ensuring that you secure the edges to a tabletop or board with masking tape as you go.

If a large piece of this fabric is not taped down in the first instance, it can adhere to anything it brushes against whether it is a person, a tabletop or other fabrics. It can be very off putting and an irritating waste of time unsticking it from all the surfaces. Once this action is completed, the possibilities offered are endless. It is easy at this stage to gently lift one edge in order to slip a paper design under the semi-transparent fabric in order for the outline placements to show through as a guide.

Threads, yarns and fabric pieces can be arranged on the sticky surface enabling a whole design structure to be built up in its entirety. At this stage it is relatively easy to lift and re-position threads or fabric pieces. Both geometric and organic arrangements can be created on the surface.

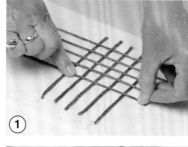

①

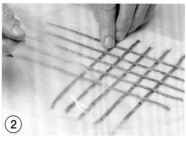

②

Once the initial set up is complete, a thin soluble film such as 'Guilietta' or' Solvy' can be placed on top and all materials pressed down firmly to stick the layers together. The masking tape around the edges can be removed at this time and the covering 'film' pressed to the edges of the base cloth. Initially, the shiny 'plastic' appearance can appear a little confusing both by its feel and the

effects of the covering film very slightly distorting the trapped, coloured threads and fabrics. Additional designs or textures can now be worked on top of the film. The huge advantage is that the double layer of soluble fabric is extremely strong enabling an amazing amount of heavy, layered or encrusted stitching to be sewn without the materials tearing.

The design can be decorated with both hand and machine stitching. Always remember that when creating a fabric using this method, all the stitching or fabrics should link one to another so the created fabric holds its shape as one piece (see Book 1 - Vanishing Act). Be aware of a false sense of security as the layered cloth appears so stable and it is easy to think that all shapes are linked. Hold the design up to the light to ensure all is progressing successfully. Bold, chunky yarns and stitches can be worked through the layers to build up a rich, encrusted or decorative surface. Machine stitching can be worked to form a holding structure before embellishing with hand stitches, wires, beads and other materials.

An extremely fragile or lacy design may need to be pinned to a piece of polystyrene or styrofoam for protection before immersing in water to wash away the base 'Aquabond' material. If a robust design has been stitched, this can be plunged into a bowl or bath of warm water. Several rinses in clear water will result in a soft fabric when dry. A little residue left in the fibres will give a stiffer finish that may be more appropriate for the particular project in hand.

The main piece on the opposite page celebrates how effective a simple grid worked in this technique can be.

The staged samples (1 & 2) show the varying actions taken and sample 3 illustrates the machine stitching worked as an under structure to link all the sections and support the weight of the double cross stitches worked in a metallic tape. The top stitch is wrapped with a twinkly crochet yarn. Beads have been added to the stitches placed at the intersections.

Continuing with the same method of fabric construction, described on the previous pages, these pieces were inspired by details taken from jewellery designs: the squared network (above) from the centre sketch and the curvy grid (right) from the drawing of the top bangle. An exciting knitting tape was used for both samples with sorbello stitch used in the first instance and single open chain and knotted cable chain stitches for the second piece. Beads decorated both.

This Page: *Old tiles on a floor within Hampton Court Palace inspired this piece. The dark but rich colours and eroded surfaces were most appealing. A range of applied materials, bonded fabric and thread snippets under polyester 'chiffon', metallic fabric paints, 'Xpandaprint' and seeding stitches were combined to interpret this embroidery.*

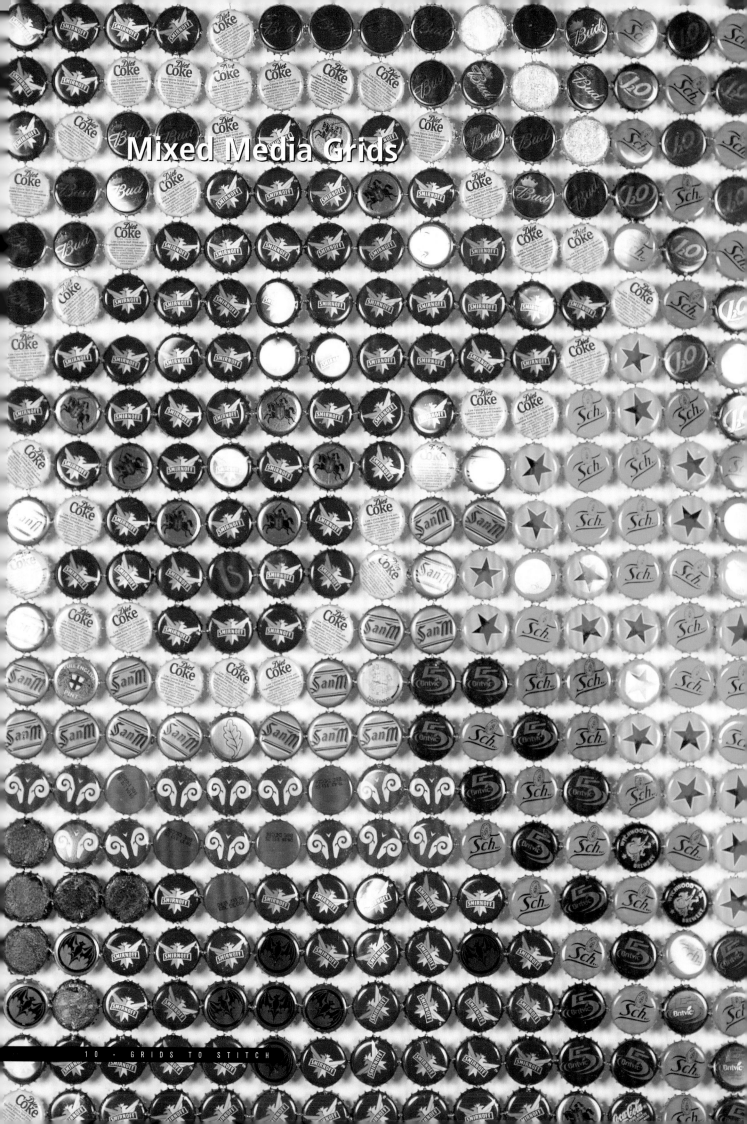

Mixed Media Grids

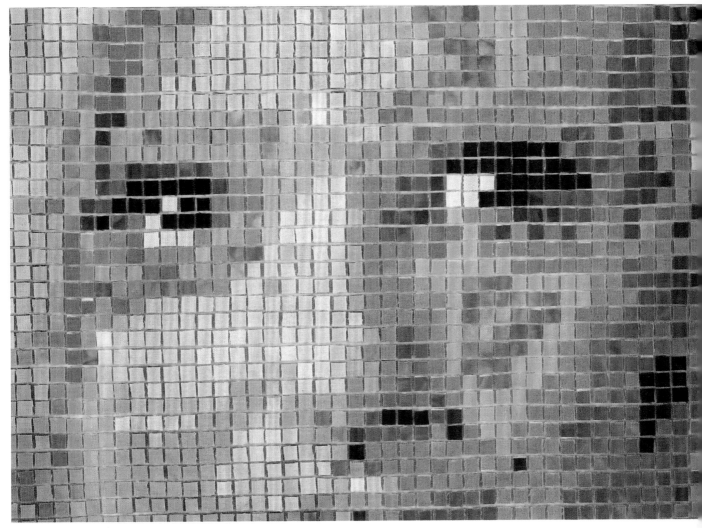

Left Page: *Bottle tops - Wired bottle tops inspired by Masai beadwork patterns. Madelaine Hutchin*

This page: *Details from 'Double Exposure' 49"x18" (125 x45 cms.)*

29,952, squares measuring 3/16" (5mm.) of hand dyed cotton fabric bonded to a sheer silk formed this fascinating double sided panel. Two photos were manipulated on the computer to create a pixalated version. A grid was drawn over the two enlarged images and placed under the sheer silk to act as a guide. Sixty different coloured fabrics cut into squares were needed to match the colours in the photographs. The action of bonding the fabric pieces back to back stabilised the whole piece. Marty Jonas. USA.

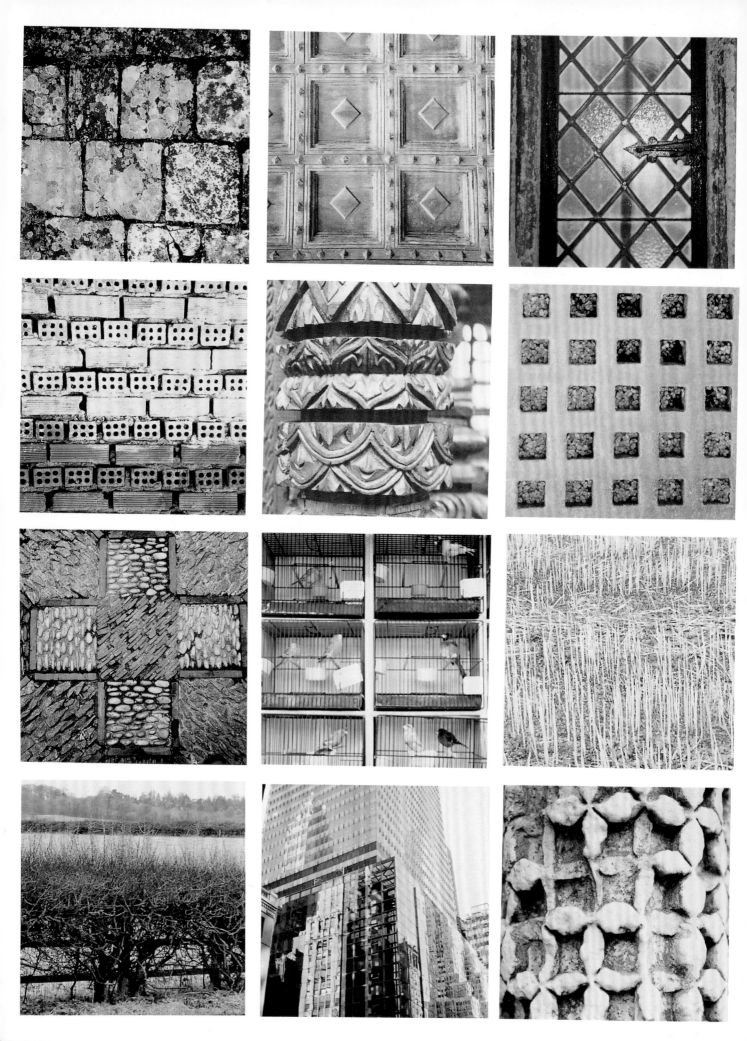

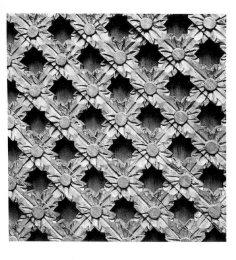

Organic Grids

Decaying honeycomb

Combs are about 3-4 cms deep
and have layers of
paper like fibre

Tree like structure forms
the stem that attaches
The comb

The hexagons

The underneath as dome shaped grids
to each individual cylinder

③

④

②

Some kind of focus helps channel constructive thought and prevent prevarication. Organic grids offer limitless possibilities ranging from strictly controlled accurate structures, through slightly less formal grids, down to 'ordered chaos'. A personal theme is a good way to become involved and immersed in a subject. Work can be developed through sustained effort and this intimate knowledge may yield worthwhile results.

Within this framework there is scope for other ideas and under a general heading of 'Pathways', grids could be an added element. A walk in a dried up riverbed in Greece revealed the extent to which grids are fundamental to our lives.

In places where the mud had become cracked in the relentless heat of the sun, the resulting shapes formed a logical if irregular grid.

Along the stone lined sides of the

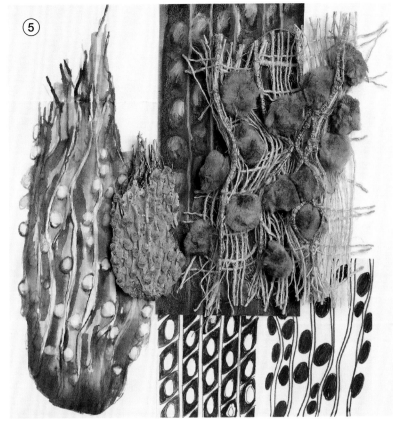

⑤

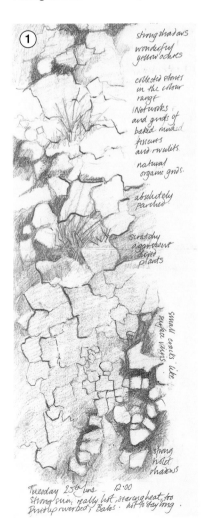

①

strong shadows
wonderful yellow ochres
collected stones in the colour range
Networks and grids of baked mud tessures and rivulets
natural organic grids.
absolutely parched
scratchy aggressive dried plants
small cracks like surface veins
strong harsh shadows

Tuesday 25th June 12.00
strong sun, really hot, searing heat, too
Dried up riverbed, Batos. Not to stay long.

dried up river were wonderful bleached out plants, herbs, seed heads and unusual pinecones. A small collection of 'found objects' served as a reminder of the walk. A set of stones was carefully selected to reflect the major colours of the riverbed. An old discarded honeycomb was an exciting find and the hexagonal structure a stunning example of a natural grid.

Dried out prickly pear fruits also littered the path. They were underpinned by fibrous grids that held the flesh together but in the heat of the sun the flesh withered away to reveal the under structure. Tiny 'pom pom' like forms clung to the sides of the dried out fruit and destroyed the symmetry as they dropped off. On the spot drawings made along the walk were hurried but contained useful notes and impressions. Despite their brevity they conveyed the sensation of the moment far more honestly than photographs. However, the digital camera was an excellent aid when confirming details for more developed studies later.

Under a magnifying glass the natural forms revealed the most amazing structures and the drawings made will be a valuable source of information in the future.

The samples on these pages were developed directly from the notes and drawings made on the walk.

1: A quick sketch made on location to establish an essence of the experience.

2: Various studies based on a found honeycomb using fine line pen, 'Koh-I-Noor' colours and water soluble pencils.

3: A honeycomb machine stitched grid, worked on soluble fabric, was dissolved and then applied to a frame before being dipped in paper pulp.

4: A piece of old newsprint served as a background for a machine grid that was then dipped in water and distressed by handling and friction.

5: Studies of the prickly pear inspired a manipulated sample describing the decay of the grid.

Grids & Distortions

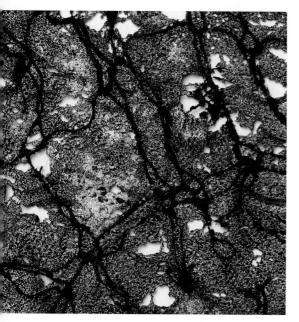

Whilst there is a pleasing symmetry about formal grids they can be even more exciting when they become distorted. Sometimes this occurs naturally, as for example, with the tiles at the bottom of a swimming pool that have marvellous irregular patterns when the water is disturbed. Photographs taken of water in different lights and at varying times of day will reveal fluid and sinuous patterns.
Regular grids reflected in shiny curved surfaces such as kettles and Christmas baubles become distorted and may be drawn or photographed.
Various computer programmes are designed to create an array of fantastic grids and have the advantage of carrying this out at great speed.
However, effective distortions may also be worked by cutting up photographs or photocopies of drawings into various configurations.

Grids drawn onto transparent acetate sheets and superimposed over designs will determine the effectiveness of rendering an image in a grid like form.

Nets of assorted grids and thicknesses will support a number of techniques. There are many commercial nets and canvases constructed from natural and synthetic materials. Appropriate darning and stitching techniques exploit the various fabric grids.
'Lacis' darning is a traditional form of net embroidery that requires a square net for its grid like characteristic.
To bring this technique up to date it is possible to construct grids and they can be tailored to specific ideas and distorted where appropriate.
Nets may also be made on soluble fabrics using machine stitching or knotting structures over a frame.
Open grids can be freely knitted and stabilised by being supported on soluble fabric and machine stitched to consolidate.
The notebook page (right) exploits stiffened knotted nets. For this technique the structure is knotted over a frame using robust, non hairy, fibres. The irregular grids are then coated with P.V.A. glue and left to dry. Once cut off the frame the structures are stiff and can be used in many ways.
The inspiration for the larger sample was an old Tunisian fishing net draped with fibrous strips of weed and accumulated detritus. Freely worked 'Lacis' darning was stitched into the squares and additional fibres wrapped and suspended.
The small sample (top left) features free darning into a found plastic net.

Synthetic materials respond to heat and this attribute is useful when distorting grids.

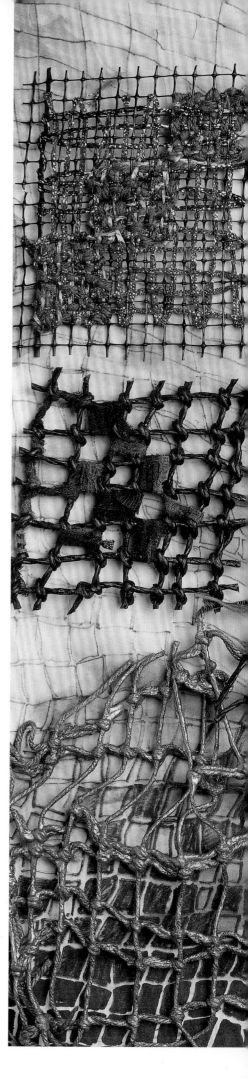

The dark grid (far left) has been knitted with synthetic fibre before being pressed onto a gilded bonded ground. The acrylic felt background offered the further possibility of distortion with a heat gun. When heating synthetic fibres in this way it is best to support them in a frame for a more controlled effect. Also remember that the fumes are toxic so wear a mask and use in a well-ventilated room or outside. The grids (right) have all been achieved with heat distortion.

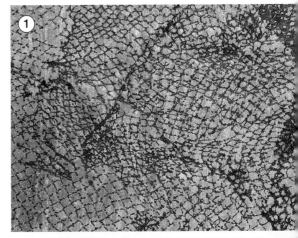

1: On a background that had been prepared with painted 'Bondaweb' and iridescent foil, black plastic grapefruit bags were ironed onto the surface under a sheet of baking parchment. This required careful handling as the plastic shrivelled quickly and needed firm pressing to ensure it adhered to the surface giving control over the melting process. Several layers of netting were applied, one at a time, to cover the ground.

2: Plastic net was first ironed between two layers of painted 'Bondaweb' and baking parchment. The shrinkage was controlled by the length of ironing time and amount of pressure.
Finally sheer nylon scarves were ironed to both sides between layers of baking parchment before using a heat tool to distress.

3: Once again a bonded background formed the ground for a melted plastic grid. This time the plastic fibres were fused into a grid by ironing between sheets of baking parchment before being stitched to the prepared background. The plastic fibres are readily available from stores that sell packets for simple braid making

For guilding and bonding techniques see Book 3 - Bonding & Beyond.

Take a piece of fabric and...

Woven fabrics have inspired numerous traditional techniques that depend on the type of fibre and nature of the weave for their successful application. Textile practice that relates directly to the nature of the background used is much more satisfying. An effective method of understanding the nature of a fabric is to experiment and treat it in a number of different ways. The point of the exercises seen here was to explore the nature of a woven cloth.

To do this it was necessary to use a piece of fabric that was large enough to cut into smaller pieces so that each could be treated differently and compared to the original.

In a workshop situation the challenge/response method works well as the students do not have preconceived ideas and work spontaneously.

The fabric used was a beautiful, textured, woven silk fabric that had been worked in different ways after being inspired by a set of words. The words were selected to encourage varying responses. Apart from the words the other overriding consideration was to be honest to the nature of the cloth and not totally overwhelm the characteristics.

Naturally this exercise could work well with many different fabrics when other aspects could be exploited.

1: In preparation the plain terracotta coloured silk was printed and sprayed with a variety of surface paints using stencils and printing blocks.

2: The first word was DECONSTRUCT and the obvious thing to do was withdraw the threads resulting in a fragile but rather atmospheric piece that resembled a really ancient fragment from a tomb.

3: ENRICH is a subtle word and, because of the nature of the weave, darning seemed ideal as it insinuated itself into the fabric. Combined with other surface stitching it allowed the fabric to retain some of its original characteristics.

4: The word ADORN invites a totally decorative approach but in this case the withdrawn threads combined with rhythmic wrapping, beads and sequins add decoration whilst remaining honest to the weave.

5: DEPTHS AND HOLLOWS can involve various methods of cutting, folding, layering and manipulation but honeycomb smocking answered the question and related to the formality of the structure.

6: RECONSTRUCT was a marvellous opportunity to use all the discarded fabrics and fibres. The 'leftovers' were arranged onto a soluble adhesive fabric (see page 2) and stitched to form a new cloth grid.

The device of using words has been successful in workshop situations but there is no reason why it should not work equally well at home and using different words. It is also a good way to encourage the combination of concept with technique.

There are many words that can be used and you can find your own but the list could include the following:

- EMBELLISH
- PRESERVE
- DISTRESS
- DECADENCE
- IMPOVERISHMENT
- MENACE
- SEDUCTIVE
- OPPULENT
- FRUGALITY
- ATTRACTIVE
- ENTICING
- COMFORTABLE
- SECURITY

Embellishing the Grid

The embellisher or needle punch machine is a really exciting tool. It can contain either five or seven barbed needles (depending on the model). There are some sewing machines on which an embellishing foot and the relevant attachments may be used.

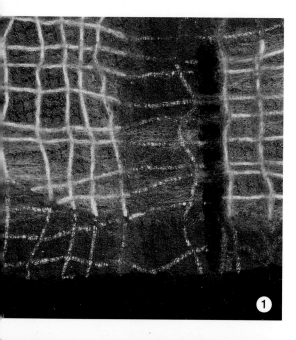

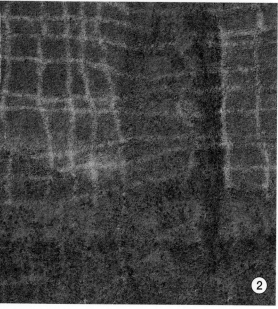

The specialised needles embed, or 'felt', fibres and fabrics into the surface.

Perhaps the name, 'embellisher', doesn't help as it implies something merely applied to a fabric and many people have dismissed it before recognising its' potential.

The applications are numerous and here it is only possible to touch on some of them.

About the size of a small sewing machine, the first astonishing thing about the embellisher is that it is so simple to use.

There are no threads or bobbins to wind and the operation could not be more straightforward. A simple adjustable pressure foot holds the fabrics down and a foot pedal works in a way similar to that of a standard sewing machine.

For a first sample an easy to use fabric such as felt is a good idea but almost any fabric may be used. It is also useful to assemble some fibres threads and fabrics to 'apply' to the surface.

i. Place the fabric on the machine bed and lower the presser foot. Depending on the thickness of the layers being used, the foot may be adjusted to high and low settings.

ii. Place another fabric on top and then press the foot pedal and move the fabric sandwich back and forth as desired. To start with it is best not to work too fast and, by experience, speed will increase. However, working too quickly can occasionally result in bent or broken needles.

iii. It is soon possible to develop a rhythm and it takes time to realise that bobbins do not have to be replaced and results happen almost as if by magic.

iv. Experiment by placing various fibres on the surface and watch them being embeded into the ground. The more a spot is worked the more fused and muted it will become.

v. Turn the fabric over and work from the back to see what happens.

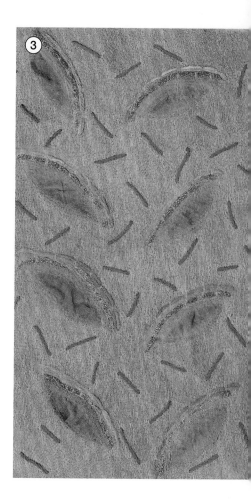

vi. Apply fibres to the reverse and embellish them into the surface. On turning it over again the 'ghosting ' of the fibres will show on the front. The intensity of the image will often be determined by the amount of working.

Thus, with a basic knowledge of the machine, further samples may be carried out on a range of thick and thin materials.

If not too intensively worked the surface additions may be easily pulled away and reapplied.

To be really secure, the manufacturers suggest working first from the front, then the back and finally the front again. In this way practical items will stand a degree of wear and tear. However, for wall hangings and backgrounds, this may not be necessary.

Among the many marvellous aspects of this machine, the possibilities for drawing on the front and back are the most exciting.

Wonderful layered atmospheric imagery is possible.

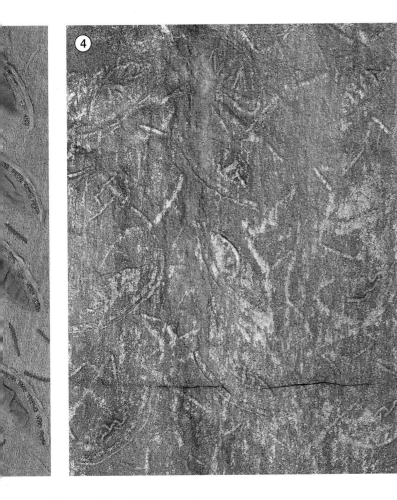

The resulting fabrics may be enhanced with machine and hand stitching and even further embellished after that for totally integrated surfaces.

1: Dyed cotton gauze was first placed over an acrylic felt and fused with the embellisher.

A synthetic net bag was embedded into the fabric and a wool grid placed over the top. Finally black velvet was worked into the image and secured firmly.

2: The reverse of the sample demonstrates the 'ghosting' of the wool grids.

3: This background was created with the embellisher. It 'felted' cotton scrim and velvet shapes into a 'pavement grid'. Hand stitching completed the texture.

4: The whole sample was then ironed with painted 'Bondaweb' and gilding foil.

5: A sheer nylon scarf was ironed to this sandwich of layers to seal the surface.

The final stage was to use the embellisher to reveal and highlight aspects of the design.

At first it was worked on the reverse to push the grid shapes through the surface and offer a contrast.

It was necessary to keep turning it over to ensure that the various elements were correctly placed.

With a complex design it may be necessary to make stitched guidelines to ensure accuracy.

Further fibres were added to the front to give the impression of metallic decay.

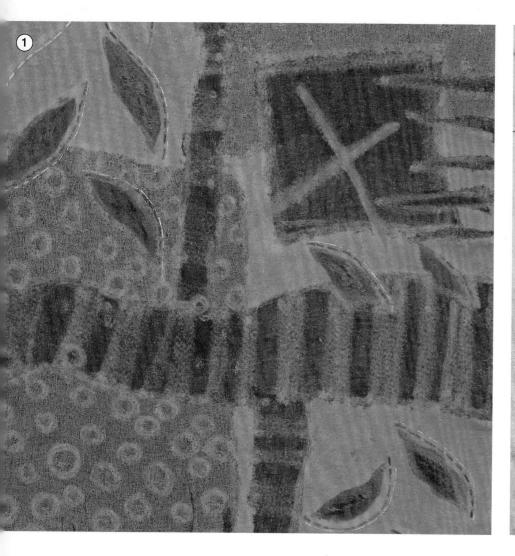

Pathways & Grids

Another definition of the word 'grid' describes it as 'a framework of parallel metal bars covering an opening, esp. a drain; a grating'. Pathways feature metal manhole covers, gratings and drain covers all containing grids.
Where the metals have corroded the colours are much less harsh and reflect subtle hues.
Pathways are also crisscrossed by the irregular grids of patches and marks resulting from years of upheaval.
On the edge of pavements there are often 'rumble strips' containing regular raised grids to inform the blind of potential danger.

Some grids are broken down by wear and tear and reflect the rhythms of daily life.
Leaves decay and insinuate themselves into the fabric of the path and blossoms and berries disrupt the grids.
In the frost and snow the patterns and colours of the grids change again.
From these observations and studies a whole series of textile pathways emerged. Much of the work featured here was worked on an embellishing machine.

1: 'X marks the Spot' (86cms x 56cms) this work celebrates the grids and markings of a well worn path. It contains references to the history of the path and the patches of pattern that are etched into it by the routine rhythms of daily life.

The background is a fusion of acrylic felt and dyed cotton scrim to which have been added a range of velvets and coloured felts. Throughout the process it was worked on the front and the back alternatively to achieve more sensitive fabric marks. Hand stitching added further detail and in parts the embellisher was also used to bed this in.

2: This detail of a path grid has been made from painted and treated felt that has been cut, manipulated and stitched to form an open textile structure. Maria Rogers

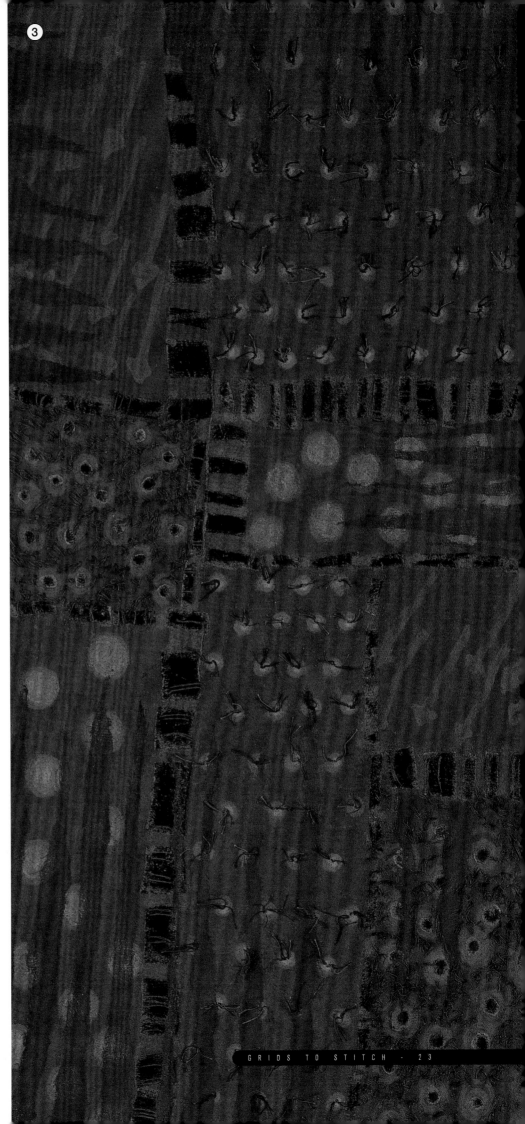

3: 'We Cast Long Shadows'
(76cms x 136cms) is another in
the 'Pathways' series and it
incorporates several techniques
using the embellishing machine.

This piece explores the notion of
a footpath as an ancient carpet
and uses a grid formation of a
woven kilim.

The patterns however are all
derived from marks found on
pathways in every day use. The
subtle colours of the fabrics were
made by over dying with a range
of dark colours to achieve the
shades found in tarmac which is
surprisingly colourful when
examined closely.

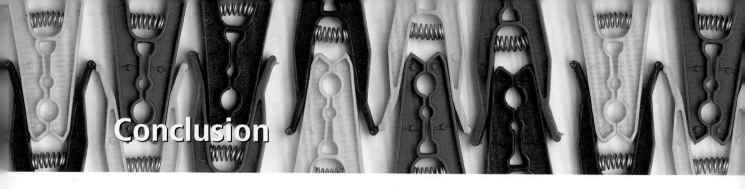

Conclusion

Some artists enjoy creating designs using mathematical formulae and the many programmes that computers can offer to repeat, invert, rotate and change the scale of chosen motifs into the most intricate grid arrangements. Positive and negative imagery, colour washes and textural marks can be added to develop the designs in a sophisticated manner. For others, this approach may not involve them emotionally.

Much fun can be had by compiling simple, but unusual, grid patterns using every day objects. Striped and checked wrapping paper can be cut and collaged into attractive designs. Alternatively, select a group of objects such as patterned sweets,

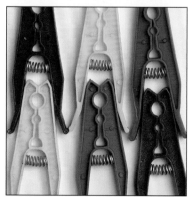

marbles, nuts and bolts, bubble wrap segments, lengths of coloured straws, small squares of cereal, clothes pegs, flower heads etc and arrange them into various grid patterns. Draw or photograph various placements and the results may be surprising. In some cases the background spaces may be the most interesting to develop into a design and different coloured backgrounds can also alter the overall effect.

Hopefully by focusing on grids, your observation skills will be sharpened. Whilst walking along streets, paving stones, varying patterned drain covers, views through mesh fences, formally planted gardens, shadows and reflections may become more interesting. Along with the other ideas suggested in this book, it is hoped that the possibilities that grids have to offer may inspire many stitched artefacts and much enjoyment.

Directing a finely tuned focus on a particular subject or element can be wholly satisfying. Details can really be seen which may not have been noticed when making casual observations.

It can be likened to an experienced chef or wine expert who, having made a long study of their profession, can differentiate between delicate flavourings whereas not all are aware of these subtle nuances. An experienced musician or dancer will also be able to appreciate a particularly sensitive or emotional rendering beyond the initial technical skills.

The ever present aim for an artist is to expand their horizons, to select the right technique to portray the idea and to interpret and display a personal slant in order to create that special something which identifies their particular style and passion for their subject.

Books to read

The Earth from the Air 365 days - Yann Arthu-Bretrand - Thames and Hudson
By Nature's Design - An Exploratorium Book - Chronicle Books SF. USA
The Elements of Design - Loan Oei and Cecile De Kegel - Thames and Hudson
Knotting and Netting - Lisa Melen - Van Nostrand Reinhold

Acknowledgements

Our sincere thanks as always go to our husbands Steve Udall and Philip Littlejohn for their continued support, to Michael Wicks, our photographer and Jason Horsburgh, our designer for their encouragement and expertise. Special thanks go to our students for allowing us to use their work and to the textile artists Marty Jonas (USA), and Hilary Hollingworth (UK).

The products and suppliers used in our books are listed at www.doubletrouble-ent.com

Double Trouble

Booklets in this series include: